HOW TO BECOME A MAGISTRATE IN THE UK

A BITE-SIZE GUIDE TO UNDERSTANDING THE ROLE AND JOINING THE JUDICIARY

BUKKY OKUNADE

This publication is intended for general information purposes only. It does not constitute legal advice or official guidance. While every effort has been made to ensure accuracy at the time of writing, laws, procedures, and guidance may change. Readers should always verify information with official sources, including guidance issued by the Judicial Office and the Magistrates' Association, before acting on it.

ISBN: 9781068465543

Dedication

For everyone who is ready to step forward and serve.

Even small actions can make a real difference in your community.

Table of Contents

Introduction 1

Chapter 1: Why the Magistracy Matters 3

Chapter 2: The Justice System and Where Magistrates Fit Within It 7

Chapter 3: What Magistrates Actually Do on the Day 11

Chapter 4: Who Can Apply to Become a Magistrate 16

Chapter 5: The Six Key Qualities and How to Evidence Them 21

Chapter 6: The Unspoken Realities of Sitting on the Bench 26

Chapter 7: Court Visits and Observations 30

Chapter 8: The Application Process Step by Step 34

Chapter 9: Interview Preparation and Scenario Practice 39

Chapter 10: Training, Mentoring, and Your First Year on the Bench 44

Chapter 11: Ethics, Impartiality, and Public Confidence 48

Chapter 12: Dealing with Challenging and Sensitive Cases 53

Chapter 13: Family Court Work, Youth Court, and Specialist Jurisdictions 58

Chapter 14: Growing in the Role and Additional Responsibilities 63

Chapter 15: A Sustained Act of Service 67

Useful Resources 70

About the Author 72

INTRODUCTION

Justices of the Peace, also known as magistrates, sit at the heart of local justice in England and Wales. They play a crucial role in maintaining law and order by making decisions on criminal, civil, and family cases. The decisions they make affect real lives in tangible ways, from upholding justice to determining sentences that can change the course of someone's life.

This role is not reserved for lawyers or legal experts. It is open to people from all walks of life, provided they possess the qualities that matter most: fairness, sound judgment, and a strong commitment to serving the community.

Magistrates work as part of a bench, usually made up of three individuals, ensuring decisions are made collectively and fairly. The bench's diversity is vital to its strength, as it brings local knowledge and perspectives to the courtroom, making justice more accessible and connected to the communities it serves.

In this guide, I'll take you through what it means to be a magistrate and provide clear steps for applying, preparing for interviews, and succeeding once you're appointed. It's a role that requires dedication but offers immense personal and professional rewards. Serving on the bench allows you to contribute meaningfully to your community, ensuring that justice is not only done but seen to be done.

Who This Guide is For

This book is for anyone considering becoming a magistrate. Whether you're interested in a role that offers real responsibility and the opportunity to make a tangible difference, or you're simply curious about the justice system, this guide will help you:

- Understand the role of a magistrate and what you'll be expected to do
- Learn about the application and selection process
- Prepare for the court observations and interviews with confidence
- Develop examples and answers to succeed in the interview process
- Build a clear plan for entering the magistracy

You don't need a legal background. What matters most is a commitment to fairness, a willingness to learn, and the ability to make decisions impartially. This guide will help you determine if this is the right path for you and give you the tools to succeed.

What You Will Get from This Guide

By the end of the book, you will have a deep understanding of the magistracy, including:

- The role of magistrates in the justice system
- Eligibility criteria and application process
- How to prepare for court observations
- How to craft strong answers for interview questions
- Scenario-based exercises to strengthen decision-making skills
- A practical step-by-step action plan for applying

This guide aims to provide the clarity you need to move forward with confidence, whether you're just starting to consider the magistracy or already preparing to apply.

Chapter 1

Why the Magistracy Matters

Public trust in the justice system depends not only on laws and procedures, but on the people who apply them. Magistrates are entrusted with making decisions that require fairness, balance, and restraint, often in situations where emotions run high and the consequences are serious. The authority of the role rests on public confidence that those sitting on the bench will act with integrity and sound judgement.

The magistracy is also one of the few areas of public life where ordinary citizens are appointed to exercise judicial responsibility. This is a deliberate and important feature of the system. It ensures that justice is informed by a range of life experiences and that decision-making remains grounded in everyday realities, while operating firmly within the law.

Understanding why the magistracy matters helps clarify what is expected of those who choose to serve. It is not a symbolic role or a casual commitment. It is a position of responsibility that requires preparation, self-awareness, and a willingness to be accountable for decisions that affect others.

The Magistracy as a Form of Public Service

Serving as a magistrate is a direct and practical form of public service. Magistrates contribute to the administration of justice by sitting in magistrates' courts and taking part in decisions that affect individuals, families, and communities on a daily basis.

Magistrates' courts deal with the majority of criminal cases in England and Wales, as well as certain family matters and preliminary hearings for more serious offences. This places magistrates at the centre of local justice and makes their contribution essential to the effective functioning of the court system.

By sitting on the bench, magistrates help ensure that justice is fair, consistent, and accessible. They bring community awareness and lived experience into the courtroom, while applying the law impartially with the support of a legal adviser.

Entering the Magistracy

For many people, the idea of becoming a magistrate arises through wider engagement with community or civic life. Exposure to public responsibility often prompts reflection on how decisions are made, how fairness is applied, and how justice operates at the local level.

The magistracy is not always a role people plan for early on. It is often discovered gradually, as individuals reflect on their values, experience, and capacity to serve. Considering the role seriously requires time and honesty, particularly given the responsibility involved.

The application and selection process is intentionally thorough. It is designed to assess judgement, fairness, independence, commitment, and the ability to work constructively with others. Successful applicants are appointed as Justices of the Peace and undertake structured training through the Judicial College before beginning to sit in court.

Over time, service in the magistracy can develop in different ways. Some magistrates focus on consistent sitting, while others go on to support colleagues through mentoring or to chair the bench. Whatever the path, the role demands sound judgement, discretion, and resilience, offering a sustained opportunity to contribute to the justice system in a measured and responsible way.

Why the Role Remains Important

The magistracy plays a vital role in maintaining public confidence in the justice system. Magistrates bring independence, balance, and community perspective to judicial decision-making.

The importance of the role includes:

- Dealing with a high volume of cases so that the courts function efficiently
- Ensuring justice is delivered locally by people drawn from the community
- Bringing a range of life experience into judicial decision-making
- Supporting fairness, transparency, and consistency in the courts

At a time when trust in public institutions cannot be taken for granted, the presence of committed, fair-minded magistrates remain essential.

A Realistic Picture of Responsibility

Becoming a magistrate involves real authority and real responsibility. It is not an honorary role.

Magistrates are expected to:

- Listen carefully to evidence and submissions
- Work constructively with other magistrates on the bench
- Reach decisions collectively, even where views initially differ
- Apply the law with the support of a legal adviser
- Maintain confidentiality at all times

Magistrates must also commit time each year to sittings and mandatory training. This requires honesty about availability and, where relevant, support from employers or family.

Is This Role Right for You

The magistracy is well-suited to people who value fairness, consistency, and service. It is not about status or influence. It is about judgement, reliability, and trust.

This role may be right for you if you:

- Care about justice and community wellbeing
- Can listen without rushing to conclusions
- Are willing to work as part of a bench
- Are open to learning and feedback
- Can commit time consistently

Confidence develops through training and experience. Commitment and integrity must be present from the start.

Chapter 2

The Justice System and Where Magistrates Fit Within It

The justice system can appear complex from the outside, particularly to those who have never been in a courtroom. Understanding where magistrates fit within that system is essential before deciding whether the role is right for you. This chapter provides a practical overview of the courts and the specific place magistrates hold within them.

Magistrates operate within a structured legal framework, supported by professional judges, legal advisers, and court staff. While magistrates are not legally qualified judges, their role carries judicial authority and responsibility. The system is designed so that magistrates apply the law with support, not in isolation.

Magistrates' Courts in England and Wales

Magistrates' courts are the foundation of the criminal justice system in England and Wales. The majority of criminal cases begin and end in these courts.

Magistrates' courts deal with:

- Summary offences, which are less serious criminal matters
- Either way offences, which may be heard in the magistrates' court or sent to the Crown Court
- Preliminary hearings for more serious offences before transfer to the Crown Court

- Certain family matters, depending on the bench and jurisdiction

These courts operate locally, serving specific geographic areas. This local connection is a key feature of the magistracy.

Sitting on the Bench

Magistrates usually sit as a bench of three. One magistrate acts as the presiding justice, chairing the bench and guiding discussions. Decisions are reached collectively.

Sitting as part of a bench means:

- No magistrate makes decisions alone
- All views are heard and considered
- Differences of opinion are discussed respectfully
- Final decisions reflect collective judgement

This collaborative approach strengthens fairness and consistency in decision-making.

The Role of the Legal Adviser

Each bench is supported by a legal adviser. The legal adviser is legally qualified and is responsible for advising magistrates on law and procedure.

The legal adviser:

- Explains relevant law and legal tests
- Advises on sentencing powers and guidelines
- Ensures correct courtroom procedure is followed

The legal adviser does not make decisions. Magistrates remain responsible for findings of fact and outcomes.

Criminal and Family Work

Magistrates may sit in different jurisdictions depending on training and appointment.

In criminal courts, magistrates deal with matters such as:

- Pleas and trials
- Bail and remand decisions
- Sentencing within their legal powers

In the family court, magistrates may deal with:

- Care and supervision matters
- Applications involving children and family responsibility

Family proceedings are often not open to the public and require specific training and sensitivity.

The Value of Local Knowledge

One of the strengths of the magistracy is the contribution of local understanding. Magistrates are not representatives of the community, but they do bring awareness of social context and lived experience into the courtroom.

This helps the bench:

- Understand the wider impact of decisions
- Consider rehabilitation and prevention alongside punishment
- Apply the law with awareness of real-world consequences

Local knowledge must always sit alongside impartiality and adherence to the law.

Working with Court Staff and Professionals

Magistrates work alongside a range of professionals, including:

- Court clerks and ushers
- Prosecutors and defence representatives
- Probation and youth offending teams
- Interpreters and support services

Effective magistrates treat all court users with courtesy and respect, recognising the importance of professionalism in maintaining confidence in the justice system.

The Challenge and Responsibility of the Role

Serving in the justice system brings challenges. Magistrates must concentrate for long periods, manage emotionally difficult material, and make decisions that may be unpopular or contested.

The responsibility lies in:

- Remaining calm and fair under pressure
- Setting aside personal views and assumptions
- Making decisions based on evidence and law
- Maintaining confidentiality and dignity at all times

These challenges are balanced by the knowledge that magistrates play a vital role in upholding justice at a local level.

Chapter 3

What Magistrates Actually Do on the Day

Understanding what happens on a sitting day is essential before applying to become a magistrate. While the role carries authority, it is also structured, supported, and collaborative. Magistrates do not work alone and are never expected to know everything from the outset.

A typical sitting day involves preparation, careful listening, discussion with fellow magistrates on the bench, and decision-making supported by legal advice. Each case is different, but the principles of fairness, impartiality, and respect remain constant.

Preparing for Court

Before court begins, magistrates review the case list and familiarise themselves with the types of hearings scheduled for the day. This preparation helps ensure that the bench is ready to focus on the issues that will arise.

Preparation involves:

- Arriving on time and ready to sit for the full session
- Reviewing the order of cases and types of hearings
- Being mentally prepared to concentrate for extended periods
- Approaching each case with an open mind

Magistrates must not conduct independent research or discuss cases outside court.

Magistrates are provided with laptops or tablets in court, which they use to view case papers, consult sentencing guidelines, and access relevant legal information during hearings. This ensures that decisions are informed, consistent, and based on current guidance.

Sitting on the Bench

Magistrates usually sit as a bench of three, with one magistrate acting as the presiding justice. The presiding justice manages the flow of the hearing and ensures that the bench works effectively together.

While sitting on the bench, magistrates:

- Listen carefully to evidence and submissions
- Observe the conduct and tone of proceedings
- Ask appropriate questions when permitted
- Take notes to support later discussion

All magistrates are equal in decision-making, regardless of who chairs the bench.

Listening and Understanding the Case

A significant part of a magistrate's role is listening. This includes listening to legal representatives, defendants, witnesses, and advice from the legal adviser.

Magistrates must be able to:

- Follow evidence and arguments accurately
- Identify relevant facts and issues
- Concentrate even when proceedings are lengthy or complex
- Remain patient and attentive throughout

Good listening underpins good judgement.

Discussing the Case and Reaching Decisions

After hearing a case, the bench will retire to discuss it privately. This discussion is a core part of the role.

During deliberations, magistrates:

- Share their views openly and respectfully
- Consider different perspectives
- Weigh evidence and credibility
- Apply legal advice appropriately

Decisions are reached collectively. Disagreement is normal and handled through discussion and reference to the law and guidance.

Working with the Legal Adviser

The legal adviser supports the bench by advising on law, procedure, and sentencing powers. Magistrates should actively seek clarification where needed.

Appropriate interactions include:

- Asking about legal tests or thresholds
- Confirming available sentencing options
- Checking procedural requirements

The final decision always rests with the magistrates.

Sentencing and Outcomes

When sentencing, magistrates must follow established guidelines and act within their legal powers. Decisions must be proportionate and reasoned.

Magistrates consider:

- The seriousness of the offence
- Aggravating and mitigating factors
- Impact on victims
- Rehabilitation, deterrence, and public protection

Clear reasons for decisions are given in open court.

Managing the Courtroom

Magistrates help maintain order and dignity in the courtroom. This is particularly important where emotions run high.

This includes:

- Remaining calm and courteous
- Addressing disruptive behaviour through proper channels
- Ensuring proceedings remain fair and respectful

The presiding justice takes the lead, with court staff supporting them.

Confidentiality and Conduct

Confidentiality is fundamental to the role. Magistrates must not discuss cases outside the courtroom or use information gained through their role for any other purpose.

Magistrates must also be mindful of:

- Public behaviour and perception
- Use of social media
- Avoiding conflicts of interest

Maintaining trust in the magistracy is a continuous responsibility.

Reflecting and Developing

After sittings, magistrates are encouraged to reflect on their performance and learning. Feedback, mentoring, and training all form part of ongoing development.

This helps magistrates:

- Build confidence and consistency
- Improve decision-making
- Stay up to date with legal changes

The role develops over time, supported by structured training and guidance.

CHAPTER 4

WHO CAN APPLY TO BECOME A MAGISTRATE

Before committing time and energy to an application, it is important to understand who can apply to become a magistrate and what is expected of candidates. The magistracy is deliberately open to a wide range of people, reflecting the communities it serves, but there are clear eligibility requirements and standards that must be met.

This chapter sets out the criteria clearly and honestly, so you can assess your suitability before moving forward.

Basic Eligibility Requirements

To apply to become a magistrate in England and Wales, you must meet the following core requirements.

Requirement	What this means in practice
Age	You must be at least 18 years old. Magistrates are usually expected to serve until at least age 70 and must retire at 75.
Residence	You should live within a reasonable distance of the court where you will sit or have strong links to the local area.
Nationality and status	British nationality is not required. You must be a legal resident and willing to take the oath or affirmation of allegiance.

Length of service	You are normally expected to commit to at least five years of service.

Time Commitment Expectations

Although magistrates serve voluntarily, the commitment is substantial and must be taken seriously.

Commitment area	Expectation
Sitting days	At least 13 full sitting days per year, or 26 half days
Training	Mandatory initial training and ongoing development
Preparation	Reading case lists and being ready to sit
Reliability	Attending sittings and training consistently

Applicants should consider how this commitment fits alongside work, caring responsibilities, and other obligations.

Character, Integrity, and Health

Magistrates are expected to meet high standards of personal conduct. Public confidence in the judiciary depends on the integrity of those appointed.

Applicants must demonstrate:

- Good character and honesty
- Respect for confidentiality
- Independence of judgement
- Emotional resilience and maturity

You must also be in good physical and mental health, able to concentrate for extended periods, and capable of dealing with potentially distressing material.

Criminal Records and Disclosures

A criminal record does not automatically disqualify someone from becoming a magistrate, but complete transparency is essential.

Consideration	How it is assessed
Minor offences	Considered in context, including how long ago they occurred
Serious offences	Likely to result in disqualification
Honesty	Complete honesty is required at all stages
DBS checks	Mandatory before appointment

Failure to disclose relevant information is more damaging than the issue itself.

Excluded Professions and Conflicts of Interest

Certain roles are incompatible with serving as a magistrate, due to conflicts of interest or the need to preserve public confidence in impartiality.

Category	Examples
Criminal justice roles	Police officers, probation officers, prison officers
Legal roles	Certain legal professionals, depending on their role and location
Other conflicts	Roles that could compromise perceived independence

If you are unsure whether your role creates conflict, this can be discussed confidentially during the application process.

The Six Key Qualities Expected of Magistrates

Selection is based on personal qualities rather than academic or professional qualifications. These qualities are assessed throughout the application and interview process.

Quality	What it looks like in practice
Good character	Integrity, discretion, and respect for confidentiality
Understanding and communication	Ability to listen, follow evidence, and communicate clearly
Social awareness	Awareness of society and the wider context of offending
Maturity and sound temperament	Calm, respectful, open-minded behaviour
Sound judgement	Logical thinking and balanced decision-making
Commitment and reliability	Willingness to give time and meet obligations

You will be expected to provide real examples that demonstrate these qualities.

Employer Support and Public Duties

If you are employed, it is important to discuss magistracy duties with your employer early.

Key points to consider:

- Magistrates are entitled to a reasonable time off for public duties
- Employers are not required to pay you while you sit
- Many employers are supportive, particularly where communication is clear

Self-employed applicants should also plan how sittings will affect their work.

Practical Readiness and Personal Circumstances

Meeting the formal eligibility criteria does not automatically mean the magistracy is the right fit at a particular time in your life. Before applying, it is important to think realistically about how the role will sit alongside your wider responsibilities.

You should consider:

- Whether you can reliably meet the minimum sitting and training requirements
- How unpaid time away from work will affect you financially
- Whether your employer or clients are likely to be supportive
- How you will manage emotionally demanding material

Many strong candidates delay applying until their circumstances allow them to commit fully. This is a sensible decision, not a failure. The magistracy benefits most from people who are ready to serve consistently and sustainably.

CHAPTER 5

THE SIX KEY QUALITIES AND HOW TO EVIDENCE THEM

The selection of magistrates is based on personal qualities rather than formal qualifications. Throughout the application, assessment, and interview stages, candidates are assessed against six key qualities. Understanding these qualities and preparing clear, relevant examples is essential.

This chapter explains each quality in practical terms and helps you think about how to evidence them from your own experience.

Overview of the Six Key Qualities

Quality	Core focus
Good character	Integrity, honesty, and discretion
Understanding and communication	Listening, comprehension, and clear expression
Social awareness	Awareness of society and the causes and impact of crime
Maturity and sound temperament	Calm, respectful, and open-minded behaviour
Sound judgement	Logical, fair, and balanced decision making
Commitment and reliability	Time commitment and dependability

Good Character

Good character underpins public confidence in the magistracy. Magistrates must have integrity in both their public and private lives.

You may be expected to show that you:

- Act honestly, even when it is inconvenient
- Respect confidentiality and sensitive information
- Avoid behaviour that could bring the magistracy into disrepute
- Maintain appropriate boundaries in personal and professional life

What interviewers look for	Examples you could use
Integrity	Situations where you acted ethically under pressure
Confidentiality	Roles involving sensitive or private information
Accountability	Owning mistakes and addressing them properly

Understanding and Communication

Magistrates must absorb information quickly, listen carefully, and communicate effectively with others in court.

You should be able to demonstrate:

- Active listening and patience
- Ability to follow complex information
- Clear, respectful communication
- Concentration over long periods

What interviewers look for	Examples you could use
Listening skills	Managing meetings or resolving disputes
Comprehension	Handling complex reports or evidence
Communication	Explaining difficult issues clearly to others

Social Awareness

Social awareness involves understanding the wider context in which offences occur, without excusing criminal behaviour.

You may show this through:

- Awareness of social issues affecting communities
- Understanding the impact of crime on victims and society
- Respect for people from different backgrounds

What interviewers look for	Examples you could use
Awareness of context	Community or voluntary work
Respect for diversity	Working with people from different backgrounds
Balanced thinking	Avoiding assumptions or stereotypes

Maturity and Sound Temperament

Magistrates must remain calm, fair, and courteous, even in difficult situations.

This includes the ability to:

- Manage emotions under pressure
- Work collaboratively with others
- Remain open-minded and respectful

What interviewers look for	Examples you could use
Emotional control	Handling conflict or difficult conversations
Teamwork	Working effectively in groups
Fairness	Treating others consistently and respectfully

Sound Judgement

Sound judgement involves weighing evidence, applying logic, and reaching balanced decisions.

You may be asked to demonstrate:

- Logical thinking and reasoning
- Ability to set aside personal bias
- Confidence in decision-making

What interviewers look for	Examples you could use
Decision making	Situations requiring careful judgement
Objectivity	Managing bias or competing viewpoints
Accountability	Standing by decisions when appropriate

Commitment and Reliability

Magistrates must commit time consistently and take their responsibilities seriously.

You should be prepared to show:

- Reliability in meeting obligations
- Willingness to prioritise public service
- Long-term commitment

What interviewers look for	Examples you could use
Time commitment	Long-term roles or responsibilities
Reliability	Consistent attendance or delivery
Motivation	Clear reasons for wanting to serve

Preparing Your Evidence

When preparing examples, focus on real experiences rather than theoretical answers.

Good examples are:

- Specific and factual
- Clearly linked to the quality being assessed
- Honest about challenges and learning
- Focused on what you did and why

Avoid exaggeration or trying to give the "perfect" answer. Authenticity matters.

Chapter 6

The Unspoken Realities of Sitting on the Bench

Much of what prospective magistrates read focuses on eligibility, procedure, and process. What is less often discussed is what it feels like to sit on the bench and carry responsibility in practice. This chapter addresses those quieter realities so that you can make a fully informed decision about whether this role is right for you.

The shift from interest to responsibility

Before appointment, the magistracy can feel theoretical. Once sworn in, the reality becomes immediate. You are no longer an observer of the process. You are responsible for decisions that affect people's liberty, family life, and future.

Even when supported by fellow magistrates and the legal adviser, the weight of responsibility is real. Recognising this shift early helps new magistrates approach the role with the seriousness it requires.

Confidence Develops Over Time

New magistrates often worry about not feeling confident enough. This is normal. Confidence is not expected at the outset and does not come from knowing all the answers.

Confidence develops through:

- Sitting regularly and observing experienced colleagues
- Asking questions of the legal adviser
- Reflecting on decisions and learning from feedback

- Accepting that uncertainty is part of careful judgement

Taking the role seriously often shows up first as caution, not certainty.

The Emotional Impact of Cases

Some cases will stay with you. You may hear distressing evidence, see repeated patterns of offending, or sit in matters involving vulnerable people and families.

What matters is how this impact is managed. Magistrates must remain compassionate without becoming overwhelmed or detached.

Helpful approaches include:

- Acknowledging emotional responses rather than suppressing them
- Using mentoring and peer support appropriately
- Maintaining clear boundaries between court and personal life

Humanity and impartiality are not opposites. They must exist together.

Collective Decision-Making on the Bench

Sitting on the bench requires humility. You will sometimes disagree with colleagues whose views are reasonable and well-informed.

Effective bench working involves:

- Listening fully to others
- Explaining your reasoning calmly
- Being open to persuasion
- Accepting collective decisions once reached

Learning when to hold your view and when to adjust it is part of developing sound judgement.

The Inconvenience of Public Service

The magistracy does not always fit neatly around work or personal life. Hearings may run longer than expected. Training may fall at busy times. Plans may need to change.

This inconvenience is part of public service. Those who manage the role best tend to accept this reality rather than resist it.

Public behaviour and personal boundaries

Once appointed, you carry the reputation of the magistracy with you. This does not require withdrawal from public life, but it does require awareness.

Magistrates must be thoughtful about:

- Conversations about crime, sentencing, and the courts
- Social media use and online commentary
- Avoiding situations that could create perceived conflicts

Maintaining public confidence is an ongoing responsibility, not a one-time consideration.

Why People Stay

Despite its challenges, many magistrates serve for decades. They stay because the role is meaningful and rooted in service rather than recognition.

Magistrates often describe:

- A strong sense of contribution
- Respect for the bench and the justice process
- Personal growth in judgement, patience, and perspective

For those suited to it, the magistracy becomes a steady and enduring form of public service.

A Final Pause Before Moving On

Before turning to court visits and the application process, it is worth asking yourself one simple question:

Are you willing to carry responsibility quietly, consistently, and without recognition?

If the answer is yes, the practical steps that follow will feel like a natural progression.

CHAPTER 7

COURT VISITS AND OBSERVATIONS

Court visits are required and essential parts of the magistrate application process. They allow you to see the role in practice and help you decide whether sitting on the bench is right for you. They also provide valuable insight that will strengthen your application and interview answers.

Why Court Visits Matter

Court observation is not a formality. It is an opportunity to understand the reality of the role before applying.

Court visits help you:

- See how magistrates conduct hearings
- Observe how the bench works together
- Understand courtroom procedure and pace
- Assess whether the environment suits you

You are required to complete at least two court visits within the 12 months before submitting your application.

Arranging your Court Visits

You can observe proceedings at any magistrates' court in England and Wales.

Step	What to do

Choose a court	Select a local magistrates' court where you may later sit
Check access	Confirm public access times and any identification requirements
Plan timing	Allow time to observe more than one type of hearing
Identify yourself	Let court staff know you are a prospective magistrate

Arriving early gives you time to settle and understand the courtroom layout.

What to Observe in Court

When observing, focus on how magistrates carry out their role rather than the detail of the law.

Area to observe	What to look for
Bench dynamics	How magistrates listen, confer, and reach decisions
Presiding justice	How the chair manages the hearing
Legal adviser	How legal advice is given and used
Court users	How defendants, witnesses, and representatives are treated
Tone and fairness	Courtesy, clarity, and control of proceedings

Take discreet notes after each session rather than during proceedings.

Types Of Hearings to Observe

Seeing a range of hearings will give you a fuller understanding of the role.

Where possible, try to observe:

- Guilty pleas
- Trials for summary offences
- Bail and remand hearings
- Sentencing hearings
- Case management hearings

Each type highlights different aspects of the magistrate's responsibilities.

Family Court Observations

If you are interested in sitting in the family court, note that family proceedings are not open to the public.

In this case, you should:

- Research the family magistrate's role in depth
- Speak to serving family magistrates where possible
- Demonstrate understanding through reading and reflection

This research can be used in place of physical observation for family court applications.

Using Your Observations in Your Application

Court visits should inform your application and interview answers.

You may be asked about:

- What you observed about the magistrate's role

- How the bench worked together
- What you found challenging or surprising
- What confirmed your interest in the role

Reflect on what you saw and how it shaped your understanding.

Professional Conduct During Visits

While observing, remember that you are a guest in a working court.

You should:

- Dress appropriately
- Switch off mobile devices
- Avoid reacting visibly to proceedings
- Respect confidentiality at all times

Your conduct reflects your suitability for the role.

Reflecting on Your Visits

After each visit, take time to reflect.

Useful questions include:

- What aspects of the role appealed to me
- What aspects felt challenging
- How did magistrates handle difficult moments
- Can I see myself sitting on the bench

Honest reflection is more valuable than trying to give a perfect answer.

CHAPTER 8

THE APPLICATION PROCESS STEP BY STEP

Applying to become a magistrate is not a quick exercise. It is deliberately thorough, and that is a good thing. The process is designed to test judgement, commitment, and readiness for responsibility, not legal knowledge.

From application to appointment, the process can take many months. Some people move through it more quickly than others, depending on vacancies in their area and how each stage progresses. What matters most is not speed, but preparation and honesty at every step.

Getting Ready to Apply

Before you begin the application, you should have already done some serious thinking. By this point, you should understand what the role involves, have reflected on your readiness, and completed your court visits or research.

If you are employed, this is also the point at which employer support becomes practical rather than theoretical. The application will ask about time commitment, and you need to be confident you can meet it.

This stage is about self-honesty. The process will test suitability later, but it works best when applicants have already tested themselves.

Completing the Application Form

The application form is completed online and is more reflective than it may seem at first. It is not asking whether you want to be a magistrate. It is asking why you are suitable for the role.

You will be asked to provide information about:

- Your background and circumstances
- Your eligibility and availability
- Your court observations or research
- Your character and conduct
- Your understanding of the role

The most important part of the form is where you are asked to demonstrate the personal qualities required of magistrates. This is not about impressive job titles or professional status. It is about judgement, integrity, communication, and reliability.

Strong applications use clear, real examples. They explain what you did, why you did it, and what it shows about how you would approach the magistracy.

You will also be asked to provide referees. Choose people who know you well enough to comment honestly on your character and reliability, not just your achievements.

What Happens After You Submit Your Application

Once submitted, your application is reviewed locally. This is not just an administrative check. It is an assessment of whether you appear suitable to move forward.

If your application progresses, you will be invited to complete an assessment stage. This usually takes the form of scenario-based questions. These are designed to see how you think, not whether you know the law.

The scenarios often feel challenging, and that is intentional. They are testing fairness, balance, and reasoning under pressure. There is rarely a perfect answer. What matters is how you weigh competing considerations and stay grounded.

The Interview Stage

If you progress beyond the assessment, you will be invited to interview. For many people, this is the most demanding part of the process.

The interview explores:

- Your motivation for becoming a magistrate
- Your understanding of the role
- How you demonstrate the required qualities
- What you learned from your court visits or research
- How you would approach difficult situations

Interviews are structured and competency focused. You are not expected to perform or impress. You are expected to be thoughtful, honest, and clear.

Interviewers are experienced and will notice rehearsed or exaggerated answers. Calm, reflective responses grounded in real experience are far more effective.

Checks and Appointment

If you are successful at the interview, further checks will follow. These include background and character checks to ensure public confidence in your appointment.

This stage can take time. Silence does not mean something has gone wrong. It usually means processes are ongoing.

Once everything is complete and appointments are formally made, you will be invited to attend a swearing-in ceremony. This is the point at which your role changes from applicant to magistrate.

Training and induction

Appointment is the beginning, not the end. New magistrates undertake structured induction and training before sitting independently.

Training covers:

- Court procedure and roles
- Decision making and reasoning
- Working effectively on the bench
- Practical courtroom skills

You will not be expected to sit unsupported. Mentoring and guidance are part of the process, particularly in your first year.

A Realistic View of the Journey

Some people apply more than once before being appointed. Others decide part way through that the timing is not right. Both outcomes are valid.

The application process is as much about helping you decide as it is about selection. Those who approach it thoughtfully tend to arrive on the bench better prepared and more confident.

Where To Check the Latest Details

While this guide focuses on understanding and preparation, application windows, forms, and local requirements can change.

You should always check the official magistrates' recruitment pages before applying to confirm:

- Current application rounds
- Local vacancies
- Application deadlines
- Any updated requirements

Use this guide to prepare well, and official sources to stay current.

Chapter 9

Interview Preparation and Scenario Practice

The interview stage is where many applicants feel the most pressure. By this point, you have already demonstrated eligibility and basic suitability. The interview is not designed to trip you up or test your legal knowledge. It is designed to understand how you think, how you behave, and whether you can be trusted with judicial responsibility.

Preparation for interview is less about rehearsing perfect answers and more about understanding yourself, your motivations, and how your experience aligns with the role.

What the Interview is Really Assessing

Although questions may vary, interviews consistently focus on the same underlying areas.

Area being assessed	What interviewers are really looking for
Motivation	Why you want to serve, and whether your reasons are realistic
Understanding of the role	Awareness of responsibility, limits, and expectations
Personal qualities	Evidence of integrity, judgement, and fairness
Reflection	Ability to learn from experience and self-assess
Decision making	How you weigh information and reach balanced conclusions

Interviewers are experienced. They listen for honesty, not performance.

Preparing your Examples Properly

Most interview questions require you to draw on past experience. Good preparation means identifying examples in advance, not scripting answers.

Choose examples that show:

- How you handled responsibility
- How you dealt with disagreement or challenge
- How you made fair decisions
- How you behaved under pressure

Your examples do not need to come from senior roles. Everyday situations often demonstrate the required qualities more clearly.

Quality	Example sources
Good character	Confidential work, ethical dilemmas, trusted roles
Communication	Resolving conflict, explaining decisions
Social awareness	Community involvement, voluntary work
Maturity	Handling difficult people or situations
Judgement	Decision-making with competing interests
Commitment	Long-term responsibilities or service

Common Interview Themes

You are likely to be asked questions around these themes.

Theme	What to focus on in your answer
Why you want to be a magistrate	Public service, not personal gain
Court observations	What you learned, not what impressed you
Fairness and bias	Awareness and willingness to challenge yourself
Team decision making	Working respectfully as part of a bench
Time commitment	Realistic planning and reliability

Avoid vague statements. Be specific and reflective.

Scenario-Based Questions

Scenario questions are designed to see how you apply judgement in unfamiliar situations. There is rarely one correct answer.

What matters is that you:

- Stay calm and measured
- Identify the key issues
- Consider fairness and procedure
- Use support appropriately

Below are examples of common scenario types and what interviewers listen for in each.

Scenario type	What interviewers listen for
Emotional distressed defendant or witness	Calmness, sensitivity, control
Conflicting evidence	Logic, caution, fairness

Disagreement on the bench	Respect, collaboration
Uncertainty about the law	Willingness to seek legal advice
Allegations of unfair treatment	Impartiality and reassurance

Example Scenario Approach

Rather than rushing to an outcome, structure your thinking.

A simple approach is:

1. Acknowledge the situation
2. Identify the issue or risk
3. Explain how you would manage it
4. Reference support from the bench or legal adviser
5. Emphasise fairness and process

This shows disciplined thinking rather than instinctive reaction.

Handling Difficult Questions

Some questions may feel uncomfortable, particularly those about sentencing, bias, or public perception.

If asked about something challenging:

- Be honest about the difficulty
- Show awareness of responsibility
- Avoid absolute statements
- Emphasise adherence to law and guidance

It is acceptable to say you would reflect, seek advice, or take time. Caution is often a strength.

Practical interview tips

- Read your application again before the interview
- Revisit your court observation notes
- Speak clearly and at a measured pace
- Take time to think before answering
- Do not guess legal answers

If the interview is online, ensure you are in a quiet space and that you are technically prepared.

After the Interview

Once the interview ends, the outcome is out of your control. Some candidates hear back quickly, others wait longer.

Regardless of outcome:

- Reflect on the experience
- Note what you learned
- Recognise that not being appointed does not mean unsuitability

Many excellent magistrates were appointed on a later application.

A Final Reminder

The interview is not about proving you are perfect. It is about showing that you are thoughtful, fair, and ready to learn.

Those qualities matter far more on the bench than polished answers. In *The Act of Service*, I write about public service as a responsibility rather than a form of recognition. That mindset is exactly what will help you approach your interview in a grounded way.

CHAPTER 10

TRAINING, MENTORING, AND YOUR FIRST YEAR ON THE BENCH

Being appointed as a magistrate is the beginning of your learning, not the end of it. No one is expected to arrive on the bench fully formed. The first year is structured, supported, and designed to help you build confidence, competence, and good judicial habits.

This chapter explains what to expect during your early period of service and how training and mentoring support you as you settle into the role.

Induction and Initial Training

New magistrates complete a structured induction programme delivered through the Judicial College and local training arrangements. Training takes place before and alongside your early sittings.

Induction training focuses on:

- Understanding the role and responsibilities of magistrates
- Court procedure and the roles of court professionals
- Decision making and judicial reasoning
- Working effectively as part of a bench

Training combines guided learning with practical discussion and observation.

Learning Through Sitting

You will begin sitting in court under supervision. Early sittings are carefully managed so that you are supported and not placed in situations beyond your experience.

In your first sittings, you will:

- Sit with experienced magistrates
- Observe how hearings are managed
- Contribute gradually to discussions
- Learn by listening and reflecting

You are encouraged to ask questions and seek clarification. Doing so shows care, not weakness.

Mentoring Support

Each new magistrate is supported by a mentor, usually an experienced magistrate from your bench. Mentoring plays a crucial role in your development during the first year.

Aspect of mentoring	How it supports you
Practical guidance	Understanding courtroom dynamics and expectations
Reflection	Talking through decisions and experiences
Confidence building	Normalising uncertainty and learning
Professional standards	Reinforcing conduct and good practice

Mentoring is a confidential and supportive relationship designed to help you grow into the role.

Developing Confidence and Judgement

Confidence develops over time through repeated experience, reflection, and feedback. Early uncertainty is common and often a sign that you are taking the role seriously.

You will gradually develop:

- Comfort with courtroom procedure
- Strong listening and note-taking habits
- Confidence contributing to bench discussions
- Balanced judgement in decision-making

There is no expectation to rush this process.

Training During your First Year

Training continues throughout your first year and beyond. It is designed to reinforce learning and respond to areas where magistrates commonly need support.

Training focus	Purpose
Decision making	Applying law and guidance consistently
Bench work	Effective collective decision-making
Communication	Managing hearings clearly and respectfully
Ethics and conduct	Maintaining impartiality and trust

Training is essential to maintaining standards and public confidence.

Feedback and Appraisal

New magistrates receive structured feedback as part of their development. This may include observations, discussions, or formal reviews.

Feedback is intended to:

- Support improvement
- Identify strengths and development areas
- Build confidence through clarity

Approaching feedback with openness is key to long-term effectiveness.

Managing the Transition

The first year involves adjustment. You are balancing learning, responsibility, and practical commitments.

Helpful approaches include:

- Sitting regularly to build continuity
- Using mentoring support actively
- Reflecting after sittings
- Allowing confidence to develop naturally

Many magistrates find the first year the most challenging and the most formative.

Looking Ahead

As you move beyond your first year, your confidence and contribution will grow. Over time, magistrates may take on additional responsibilities, such as chairing the bench or mentoring others.

The early investment in training and reflection lays the foundation for effective service over many years.

CHAPTER 11

ETHICS, IMPARTIALITY, AND PUBLIC CONFIDENCE

Ethics sit at the heart of the magistracy. Public confidence in the justice system depends on the belief that decisions are made fairly, independently, and without personal influence. This chapter sets out the ethical responsibilities that shape how magistrates think, behave, and are perceived, both in and out of court.

Ethical awareness is not an abstract concept. It affects everyday decisions, from whether you should sit on a case to how you conduct yourself in public. Understanding these responsibilities early helps protect you and the integrity of the bench.

Impartiality and Fairness

Impartiality means approaching every case with an open mind and deciding solely on the evidence and the law. It requires constant self-awareness and a willingness to challenge assumptions.

Impartiality involves:

- Treating all parties with equal courtesy and respect
- Listening without pre-judgement
- Setting aside personal opinions and experiences
- Applying the law consistently

Bias can be conscious or unconscious. Recognising this is not a weakness. It is a professional responsibility.

Ethical focus	What it looks like in practice
Open mindedness	Waiting to hear all evidence before forming views
Self-awareness	Noticing personal reactions and checking them
Consistency	Applying the same standards to every case
Respect	Ensuring all court users feel heard

Conflicts of Interest

A conflict of interest arises where your impartiality could reasonably be questioned. This includes both actual conflicts and situations that may be perceived as conflicts.

You should not sit on a case where:

- You know the defendant, witness, or victim
- You have prior involvement in the matter
- Your work or voluntary role creates a connection
- A reasonable observer might question your independence

If in doubt, declare the issue. It is better to step aside than to risk undermining confidence.

Situation	Appropriate action
You recognise a name	Raise it immediately with the legal adviser
You have indirect knowledge	Declare and seek guidance
Unsure if it matters	Always declare and ask

Confidentiality

Confidentiality is fundamental to judicial trust. Information heard in court must never be discussed outside the courtroom or used for any other purpose.

This includes:

- Case details
- Deliberations of the bench
- Personal information about court users

The obligation of confidentiality continues beyond the conclusion of a case.

Conduct in and Out of Court

Magistrates are expected to uphold the dignity of the role both on and off the bench. This does not mean withdrawing from everyday life, but it does require awareness of how behaviour may be perceived.

Key considerations include:

- Maintaining courtesy and restraint in public settings
- Avoiding discussions about sentencing or specific cases
- Being thoughtful about opinions shared publicly

Your conduct contributes to how the magistracy is viewed as a whole.

Social Media and Public Commentary

Social media presents particular challenges. Comments made online can be taken out of context and may appear to express bias or political views.

Magistrates should be cautious about:

- Commenting on criminal justice issues
- Expressing strong views on sentencing or policy
- Sharing content that could suggest partiality

Online behaviour	Why it matters
Public posts	Can be read as personal bias
Likes and shares	May imply endorsement
Heated debate	Risks undermining neutrality

When in doubt, restraint is the safest option.

Working Ethically on the Bench

Ethical practice is reinforced through collective working. Bench discussions should be respectful, confidential, and focused on reaching a fair decision.

This includes:

- Listening to differing views
- Challenging respectfully
- Accepting collective outcomes

Disagreement handled well strengthens decision-making.

Upholding Public Confidence

Every interaction in court contributes to public confidence. People may leave court dissatisfied with the outcome, but they should leave believing they were treated fairly.

Public confidence is supported when magistrates:

- Explain decisions clearly
- Maintain calm and courtesy
- Demonstrate independence and consistency

Ethical behaviour is not about perfection. It is about care, awareness, and accountability.

When to Seek Guidance

Ethical questions will arise throughout your service. Seeking guidance is a sign of professionalism.

You can seek support from:

- The legal adviser
- The presiding justice
- Your mentor or bench chairman

Judicial ethics are upheld through shared responsibility and open discussion.

Chapter 12

Dealing with Challenging and Sensitive Cases

Some cases are straightforward. Others are complex, emotionally demanding, or involve vulnerable people and distressing facts. Dealing with challenging and sensitive cases is part of the reality of sitting on the bench, and preparation is as much about mindset as it is about procedure.

This chapter focuses on how magistrates approach difficult material with fairness, care, and professionalism, while protecting both the integrity of the court and their own wellbeing.

Understanding What Makes a Case Challenging

A case may be challenging for different reasons. It is not always the seriousness of the offence. It may be the people involved, the evidence presented, or the wider circumstances.

Common sources of difficulty include:

- Vulnerable defendants or witnesses
- Allegations involving domestic abuse or safeguarding concerns
- Conflicting or unclear evidence
- Repeated offending and entrenched behaviour
- Strong emotions in the courtroom

Recognising why a case feels challenging helps you respond thoughtfully rather than reactively.

Vulnerable Defendants and Witnesses

Many people who appear in magistrates' courts are vulnerable in some way. This may relate to age, health, language, disability, or personal circumstances.

Magistrates must balance compassion with fairness.

Situation	What magistrates focus on
Mental health concerns	Ensuring understanding and appropriate support
Learning difficulties	Clear communication and patience
Language barriers	Proper use of interpreters
Young or anxious witnesses	Sensitivity and calm courtroom management

Support measures are in place to ensure proceedings are fair. Using them appropriately is part of sound judicial practice.

Cases Involving Domestic Abuse and Safeguarding

Cases involving domestic abuse, child protection, or safeguarding can be particularly demanding. They often involve complex relationships, fear, and ongoing risk.

In these cases, magistrates must:

- Focus on evidence and legal thresholds
- Avoid assumptions or stereotypes
- Consider safety and protection carefully
- Remain calm and respectful throughout

Strong feelings are natural, but decisions must remain grounded in law and guidance.

Managing Emotional Evidence

Witnesses may become distressed when giving evidence. Defendants may express anger, fear, or frustration. Emotions do not undermine the process, but they do require careful handling.

Magistrates support fairness by:

- Allowing appropriate pauses or breaks
- Maintaining a calm and steady tone
- Ensuring everyone understands what is happening
- Avoiding behaviour that escalates emotion

The presiding justice leads this approach, supported by court staff.

Conflicting Evidence and Credibility

Some of the most challenging cases involve conflicting accounts. Magistrates must assess credibility carefully and fairly.

This involves:

- Listening closely to what is said
- Considering consistency and plausibility
- Weighing evidence as a whole, not in isolation
- Avoiding reliance on demeanour alone

Uncertainty should be acknowledged. Decisions must be based on the standard of proof and legal tests, not instinct.

Repeated Offending and Difficult Decisions

Seeing the same individuals return to court can be frustrating. It may raise questions about effectiveness, fairness, or public protection.

Magistrates must remain focused on:

- The facts of the current case
- Relevant sentencing guidance
- The balance between rehabilitation and deterrence
- Acting within legal powers

Personal frustration should never drive decisions.

Managing Personal Reactions

Magistrates are human. Some cases will provoke strong reactions. The discipline of the role lies in recognising those reactions without allowing them to influence decisions.

Helpful approaches include:

- Noticing emotional responses and setting them aside
- Discussing concerns respectfully during bench deliberations
- Seeking guidance from the legal adviser when unsure
- Reflecting after sittings rather than during hearings

Professionalism includes knowing when to pause internally.

Support and Self-Care

Support structures exist for a reason. Using them is part of responsible service.

Source of support	Purpose

Bench colleagues	Shared reflection and perspective
Mentors	Guidance and reassurance
Training	Building confidence and skill
Personal boundaries	Maintaining balance outside the court

Maintaining wellbeing is essential for sustained, effective service.

Staying Grounded in Fairness

Challenging cases test judgement, patience, and resilience. They also reaffirm the importance of the magistracy.

Remaining grounded means:

- Returning to principles of fairness and law
- Trusting the collective strength of the bench
- Accepting that not all outcomes will feel comfortable
- Knowing that careful process matters

Dealing well with complex cases is not about emotional detachment. It is about steady, principled decision-making.

CHAPTER 13

FAMILY COURT WORK, YOUTH COURT, AND SPECIALIST JURISDICTIONS

As magistrates gain experience, some choose to sit in specialist jurisdictions where the nature of the work, the people involved, and the approach required differ from the adult criminal court. Two of the most significant specialist areas are the family court and the youth court.

This chapter explains the nature of these jurisdictions, how they differ from general criminal court work, and what to consider if you are interested in developing your service in these areas.

Family Court Work

Family court magistrates deal with cases involving children and families where concerns have been raised about care, protection, or welfare. The purpose of the court is not punishment, but decision-making in the best interests of the child.

Family court work may involve:

- Applications relating to the care or supervision of children
- Decisions about where a child should live
- Safeguarding and protection concerns
- Working with reports from local authorities and professionals

The outcomes of family court cases can shape a child's life for many years, which is why the role carries significant responsibility.

How Family Court Differs from Criminal Court

Family court proceedings differ in structure, purpose, and tone from criminal cases.

Aspect	Criminal court	Family court
Purpose	Determining guilt and sentence	Protecting the welfare of children
Proceedings	Usually open to the public	Private and confidential
Focus	Offence and accountability	Best interests of the child
Evidence	Witness evidence and submissions	Reports, assessments, and professional input

Because proceedings are private, confidentiality in family court work is especially strict.

Sitting as a Family Magistrate

Family magistrates sit as part of a bench and are supported by a legal adviser, as in a criminal court. Decisions are reached collectively and are guided by law, evidence, and professional assessments.

Family magistrates must be able to:

- Read and absorb detailed written reports
- Listen carefully to complex and emotional information
- Ask clear and thoughtful questions
- Make balanced decisions in difficult circumstances

The work can be emotionally demanding and requires patience, focus, and resilience.

Confidentiality and Discretion in Family Work

Confidentiality in family court is absolute. Information heard in proceedings must never be discussed outside court.

This includes:

- Details about children and families
- Professional reports and assessments
- Bench discussions and deliberations

Family court magistrates must be particularly careful in everyday conversations and online spaces, as even indirect references could compromise privacy.

Youth Court Work

Some magistrates also sit in the youth court, which deals with cases involving children and young people aged between 10 and 17. Youth court work requires additional training and a specific approach, as proceedings are adapted to ensure that young defendants can understand and participate effectively.

Youth court magistrates balance accountability with an awareness of safeguarding, development, and rehabilitation. The emphasis is on helping young people understand the consequences of their actions while also considering their welfare and long-term prospects.

Youth court proceedings differ from adult criminal court in several ways:

Aspect	Adult criminal court	Youth court

Defendants	Adults	Children and young people aged 10–17
Approach	Formal and procedural	Adapted, accessible, and supportive
Focus	Punishment and deterrence	Accountability, support, and rehabilitation
Environment	Public courtroom	Usually closed and less formal

Youth court work can be demanding and is not suitable for everyone. It requires patience, sensitivity, and the ability to communicate clearly with young people and their families.

Training and Suitability for Specialist Work

Not all magistrates sit in family or youth courts. Additional training is required, and appointments depend on local needs and individual suitability.

You may enter specialist work in different ways:

- Applying directly to family or youth court, where vacancies exist
- Beginning in criminal court and later moving into specialist jurisdictions

Training prepares magistrates for the distinct responsibilities and ethical considerations of these courts.

Is Specialist Work Right for You

Specialist jurisdictions are not a progression in status. They are a different form of service that requires particular strengths.

You may be well-suited to family or youth court work if you:

- Can manage emotionally charged material calmly

- Are comfortable working with detailed reports and assessments
- Can maintain strict confidentiality
- Are motivated by safeguarding and long-term outcomes

Equally, choosing to remain in adult criminal court work is a valid and valuable contribution.

Making Informed Choices Over Time

Many magistrates take time before deciding whether specialist work is right for them. Experience, reflection, and honest self-assessment are important.

The magistracy benefits from magistrates serving where they are most effective, not where they feel pressured to go.

CHAPTER 14

GROWING IN THE ROLE AND ADDITIONAL RESPONSIBILITIES

For many magistrates, the role develops gradually. With experience comes confidence, perspective, and a deeper understanding of how the bench works. Growth in the magistracy is not about promotion in the traditional sense. It is about readiness to take on additional responsibility in service of the court and the people it serves.

This chapter looks at how magistrates grow into the role over time and the additional responsibilities some choose to take on.

Developing Confidence Through Experience

Confidence as a magistrate comes from sitting regularly, reflecting on decisions, and learning from others. Over time, magistrates become more comfortable with procedure, discussion, and judgement.

This development often includes:

- Greater ease in following hearings
- Stronger contributions to bench discussions
- Increased confidence in applying guidance
- Better management of personal reactions

Growth is gradual and varies between individuals.

Chairing the Bench

Some experienced magistrates go on to act as the presiding justice, often referred to as chairing the bench. This role involves guiding proceedings and ensuring that the bench works effectively.

Responsibilities of the presiding justice include:

- Managing the flow of the hearing
- Ensuring all magistrates participate
- Maintaining courtroom order and an appropriate tone
- Supporting fair and efficient decision making
- Making formal pronouncements in court on behalf of the bench, including delivering decisions and sentences

Chairing requires calm authority, good communication, and the ability to balance leadership with collaboration.

Sitting in the Crown Court

With experience and additional training, some magistrates may sit in the Crown Court as part of a mixed bench, hearing appeals from magistrates' courts or dealing with sentencing matters committed from the lower court.

In these cases, magistrates sit alongside a Crown Court judge and bring their experience of summary justice to the proceedings. This work is undertaken only by suitably trained and experienced magistrates and is not a routine part of service for all.

Mentoring and Supporting Others

As experience grows, many magistrates choose to support others through mentoring. This may involve guiding newly appointed magistrates or supporting colleagues through development.

Mentoring involves:

- Offering practical guidance
- Sharing experience and reassurance
- Encouraging reflection and confidence
- Reinforcing ethical standards

Mentoring is an essential way of sustaining quality and culture within the magistracy.

Training and Development Roles

Some magistrates contribute to training and development, supporting others' learning through structured programmes or local initiatives.

These roles may include:

- Assisting with induction training
- Supporting observation and feedback
- Sharing experience in training sessions

Such roles help ensure consistency and high standards across the bench.

Committee and Leadership Roles

Beyond sitting in court, magistrates may take on responsibilities that support the wider operation of the bench or magistracy.

This may involve:

- Contributing to bench meetings
- Supporting local leadership structures
- Representing the bench in appropriate forums

These roles require discretion, judgement, and a strong commitment to service.

Knowing When to Step Forward or Step Back

Not all magistrates wish to take on additional responsibilities, and that is entirely appropriate. Effective service includes knowing your strengths, limits, and changing circumstances.

There may also be times when stepping back, reducing sittings, or changing focus is the right decision.

Sustained service depends on:

- Honest self-assessment
- Respect for personal wellbeing
- Willingness to adapt over time

The magistracy benefits from magistrates who serve thoughtfully, not those who feel compelled to progress.

Long-Term Contribution

Many magistrates serve for decades. Over time, the role shapes how they think about fairness, responsibility, and public life.

Long-term service often brings:

- Deep understanding of the justice process
- Measured judgement
- Quiet leadership
- Consistent contribution to the community

Growth in the role is less about recognition and more about a steady, reliable presence.

Chapter 15

A Sustained Act of Service

Becoming a magistrate is not a single decision. It is a sustained commitment to fairness, responsibility, and quiet public service. Long after the application forms and interviews are complete, the essence of the role remains the same: listening carefully, judging fairly, and acting with integrity.

This guide outlines what the magistracy entails, from eligibility and training to ethics, challenging cases, and long-term service. What remains is a personal decision about whether this form of service aligns with who you are and how you wish to contribute.

Service Without Recognition

Magistrates do not seek attention. Most decisions are made out of sight, and much of the work goes unnoticed. Yet the impact is real. For those who appear in court, the experience can be life-changing.

Service in the magistracy is about:

- Carrying responsibility without status
- Making decisions collectively rather than individually
- Accepting accountability quietly
- Serving consistently over time

This is not a role for those seeking influence or visibility. It is for those prepared to serve faithfully.

Judgement Shaped by Humility

Good judgement in the magistracy is shaped by humility. No magistrate has all the answers. Decisions are reached through listening, discussion, and careful application of the law.

Over time, many magistrates find that the role deepens their understanding of people, circumstances, and consequences. This growth does not make decisions easier, but it does make them more thoughtful.

The Personal Cost and the Personal Gain

The magistracy requires time, emotional energy, and discipline. Some cases will stay with you. Some decisions will be uncomfortable. These realities should not be understated.

At the same time, many magistrates speak of:

- A strong sense of contribution
- Respect for the justice process
- Personal growth in judgement and patience
- The quiet satisfaction of service

Both the cost and the gain are part of the role.

Choosing When and How to Serve

Not everyone who reads this guide will go on to apply. Some may decide the timing is not right. Others may return to the idea later in life.

Choosing not to apply now, or at all, is not a failure. Responsible public service includes knowing when your circumstances, temperament, or priorities align with the role.

A Place within Public Life

The magistracy sits alongside other forms of public service, including local government, voluntary leadership, and national roles. It is one of the most grounded ways to contribute to the justice system.

For those who serve, the role often becomes a steady presence rather than a defining identity. It is something you do carefully and consistently, not something you promote.

Closing Reflection

In *The Act of Service*, I describe public roles as positions of trust rather than platforms for recognition. The magistracy reflects this principle in its purest form.

If you choose to pursue this path, do so with care, humility, and commitment. If you do not, let the values of fairness and responsibility still shape how you engage with public life.

Either way, understanding the magistracy deepens our collective respect for justice and those who serve within it.

Useful Resources

The magistracy and the justice system evolve over time. While this guide focuses on understanding the role and preparing thoughtfully, you should always check official sources for the most current information before applying.

The following resources are reliable starting points.

Magistrates' Judiciary	The official site for magistrate recruitment, guidance, and training. You can find information on: • Eligibility and vacancies • The application process • Court visits and research • Training and development Website: magistrates.judiciary.uk
GOV.UK – Become a Magistrate	This page provides a clear overview of: • Who can apply • What magistrates do • Time commitment and public duties • How to apply Website: gov.uk/become-magistrate
Magistrates' Association	The Magistrates' Association is a membership body that supports magistrates and provides insight into the role.

<table>
<tr><td></td><td>It offers:<ul><li>Information about magistrates' work</li><li>Training and development resources</li><li>Articles and commentary on the justice system</li></ul>Website: magistrates-association.org.uk</td></tr>
<tr><td>Court observation</td><td>To observe magistrates' court proceedings, check local court listings via:

Website: gov.uk/find-court-tribunal

Always follow court guidance on public access and conduct.</td></tr>
</table>

About the Author

Bukky Okunade is a long-serving magistrate with over twenty years of experience in the justice system. She was appointed as a Justice of the Peace in 2002 and has served across a wide range of cases, including sitting as a presiding justice and mentoring new magistrates.

Alongside her judicial service, Bukky has worked extensively in community development, public leadership, and mentoring. Her work has focused on encouraging thoughtful participation in public life and on supporting individuals in stepping into roles of responsibility with confidence, integrity, and clarity.

Bukky is the author of The Act of Service: Your Guide to Public Roles and Becoming Influential in the UK and the Guide to Public Roles series. Her writing is grounded in lived experience and reflects a belief that public service is most effective when it is approached with care, reflection, and a long-term sense of responsibility.

Further Reading by the Same Author

If you would like to explore public service and leadership in a broader context, *The Act of Service: Your Guide to Public Roles and Becoming Influential in the UK* offers reflections on responsibility, purpose, and the mindset required for roles that involve influence and decision-making. It is suitable for anyone considering public or civic roles at any level.

Other Books in the Guide to Public Roles Series

The *Guide to Public Roles* series is created to help people step into meaningful public and community service with clarity and confidence. Each book offers practical, straightforward guidance on taking on roles that support and strengthen communities across the United Kingdom.

Titles in the series include:

1. **How to Become a School Governor in the UK**
   A practical introduction to serving in education and supporting school leadership.
2. **How to Become an MP in the UK**
   A step-by-step path to understanding the journey into parliamentary service.
3. **How to Become a Councillor in the UK**
   A clear and encouraging guide for anyone interested in local government.
4. **How to Become a Charity Trustee in the UK**
   Understanding governance, responsibility, and service within the charity sector.
5. **How to Become a Non-Executive Board Member in the UK**
   An accessible guide to preparing for board roles and public appointments.
6. **How to Set Up a Charitable Organisation in the UK**
   Guidance for founders who want to create a purposeful and compliant charity.
7. **How to Get Funding for Your Charity in the UK**
   Essential strategies for finding, applying for, and securing financial support.

More titles will be added to the series to continue supporting the next generation of public and civic leaders.

www.ingramcontent.com/pod-product-compliance
Lightning Source LLC
LaVergne TN
LVHW090429210926
848480LV00002B/747

* 9 7 8 1 0 6 8 4 6 5 5 4 3 *